Art Course Logbook

ART COURSE
LOGBOOK

Date.........................

INDEX

INDEX

INDEX

INDEX

NAME OF COURSE/TUTORIAL _____

TUTOR _____ EXPIRY DATE _____

LOCATION, web address,
computer folder, book etc _____

SOFTWARE (if applicable) _____

MATERIALS

_____

_____

_____

_____

_____

_____

_____

_____

_____

_____

PROCESS

Continued on page

NAME OF COURSE/TUTORIAL _____

TUTOR _____ EXPIRY DATE _____

LOCATION, web address,
computer folder, book etc _____

SOFTWARE (if applicable) _____

MATERIALS

_____
_____
_____
_____
_____
_____
_____
_____
_____

PROCESS

Continued on page

NAME OF COURSE/TUTORIAL _____

TUTOR _____ EXPIRY DATE _____

LOCATION, web address,
computer folder, book etc _____

SOFTWARE (if applicable) _____

MATERIALS

_____
_____
_____
_____
_____
_____
_____
_____
_____
_____

PROCESS

Continued on page

NAME OF COURSE/TUTORIAL _____

TUTOR _____ EXPIRY DATE _____

LOCATION, web address,
computer folder, book etc _____

SOFTWARE (if applicable) _____

MATERIALS

_____

_____

_____

_____

_____

_____

_____

_____

_____

PROCESS

Continued on page

NAME OF COURSE/TUTORIAL _____

TUTOR _____ EXPIRY DATE _____

LOCATION, web address,
computer folder, book etc _____

SOFTWARE (if applicable) _____

MATERIALS

_____
_____
_____
_____
_____
_____
_____
_____
_____

PROCESS

Continued on page

NAME OF COURSE/TUTORIAL _____

TUTOR _____ EXPIRY DATE _____

LOCATION, web address,
computer folder, book etc _____

SOFTWARE (if applicable) _____

MATERIALS

_____
_____
_____
_____
_____
_____
_____
_____
_____

PROCESS

Continued on page

NAME OF COURSE/TUTORIAL _____

TUTOR _____ EXPIRY DATE _____

LOCATION, web address,
computer folder, book etc _____

SOFTWARE (if applicable) _____

MATERIALS

_____
_____
_____
_____
_____
_____
_____
_____
_____

PROCESS

Continued on page

NAME OF COURSE/TUTORIAL _____

TUTOR _____ EXPIRY DATE _____

LOCATION, web address,
computer folder, book etc _____

SOFTWARE (if applicable) _____

MATERIALS

_____

_____

_____

_____

_____

_____

_____

_____

_____

_____

PROCESS

Continued on page

NAME OF COURSE/TUTORIAL _____

TUTOR _____ EXPIRY DATE _____

LOCATION, web address,
computer folder, book etc   _____

SOFTWARE (if applicable)   _____

MATERIALS

_____
_____
_____
_____
_____
_____
_____
_____
_____
_____

PROCESS

Continued on page

NAME OF COURSE/TUTORIAL _____

TUTOR _____ EXPIRY DATE _____

LOCATION, web address,
computer folder, book etc _____

SOFTWARE (if applicable) _____

MATERIALS

_____
_____
_____
_____
_____
_____
_____
_____
_____

PROCESS

Continued on page

NAME OF COURSE/TUTORIAL _____

TUTOR _____ EXPIRY DATE _____

LOCATION, web address,
computer folder, book etc _____

SOFTWARE (if applicable) _____

MATERIALS

_____

_____

_____

_____

_____

_____

_____

_____

_____

PROCESS

Continued on page

NAME OF COURSE/TUTORIAL _____

TUTOR _____ EXPIRY DATE _____

LOCATION, web address,
computer folder, book etc _____

SOFTWARE (if applicable) _____

MATERIALS

_____
_____
_____
_____
_____
_____
_____
_____
_____

PROCESS

Continued on page

NAME OF COURSE/TUTORIAL _____

TUTOR _____ EXPIRY DATE _____

LOCATION, web address,
computer folder, book etc _____

SOFTWARE (if applicable) _____

MATERIALS

_____
_____
_____
_____
_____
_____
_____
_____
_____
_____

PROCESS

Continued on page

NAME OF COURSE/TUTORIAL _____

TUTOR _____ EXPIRY DATE _____

LOCATION, web address,
computer folder, book etc _____

SOFTWARE (if applicable) _____

MATERIALS

_____
_____
_____
_____
_____
_____
_____
_____
_____
_____

PROCESS

Continued on page

NAME OF COURSE/TUTORIAL _____

TUTOR _____ EXPIRY DATE _____

LOCATION, web address,
computer folder, book etc   _____

SOFTWARE (if applicable)   _____

MATERIALS

_____
_____
_____
_____
_____
_____
_____
_____
_____

PROCESS

Continued on page

NAME OF COURSE/TUTORIAL _____

TUTOR _____ EXPIRY DATE _____

LOCATION, web address,
computer folder, book etc _____

SOFTWARE (if applicable) _____

MATERIALS

_____

_____

_____

_____

_____

_____

_____

_____

_____

PROCESS

Continued on page

NAME OF COURSE/TUTORIAL _____

TUTOR _____ EXPIRY DATE _____

LOCATION, web address,
computer folder, book etc _____

SOFTWARE (if applicable) _____

MATERIALS

_____

_____

_____

_____

_____

_____

_____

_____

_____

PROCESS

Continued on page

NAME OF COURSE/TUTORIAL _____

TUTOR _____ EXPIRY DATE _____

LOCATION, web address,
computer folder, book etc _____

SOFTWARE (if applicable) _____

MATERIALS

_____
_____
_____
_____
_____
_____
_____
_____
_____
_____

PROCESS

_____
_____
_____
_____
_____
_____
_____

Continued on page

NAME OF COURSE/TUTORIAL _____

TUTOR _____ EXPIRY DATE _____

LOCATION, web address,
computer folder, book etc _____

SOFTWARE (if applicable) _____

MATERIALS

PROCESS

Continued on page

NAME OF COURSE/TUTORIAL _____

TUTOR _____ EXPIRY DATE _____

LOCATION, web address,
computer folder, book etc _____

SOFTWARE (if applicable) _____

MATERIALS

_____

_____

_____

_____

_____

_____

_____

_____

_____

_____

PROCESS

Continued on page

NAME OF COURSE/TUTORIAL _____

TUTOR _____ EXPIRY DATE _____

LOCATION, web address,
computer folder, book etc   _____

SOFTWARE (if applicable)   _____

MATERIALS

_____

_____

_____

_____

_____

_____

_____

_____

_____

_____

PROCESS

_____

_____

_____

_____

_____

_____

_____

_____

Continued on page

NAME OF COURSE/TUTORIAL _____

TUTOR _____ EXPIRY DATE _____

LOCATION, web address,
computer folder, book etc _____

SOFTWARE (if applicable) _____

MATERIALS

_____
_____
_____
_____
_____
_____
_____
_____
_____
_____

PROCESS

Continued on page

NAME OF COURSE/TUTORIAL _____

TUTOR _____ EXPIRY DATE _____

LOCATION, web address,
computer folder, book etc _____

SOFTWARE (if applicable) _____

MATERIALS

_____
_____
_____
_____
_____
_____
_____
_____
_____

PROCESS

Continued on page

NAME OF COURSE/TUTORIAL _____

TUTOR _____ EXPIRY DATE _____

LOCATION, web address,
computer folder, book etc _____

SOFTWARE (if applicable) _____

MATERIALS

_____
_____
_____
_____
_____
_____
_____
_____
_____

PROCESS

Continued on page

NAME OF COURSE/TUTORIAL _____

TUTOR _____ EXPIRY DATE _____

LOCATION, web address,
computer folder, book etc _____

SOFTWARE (if applicable) _____

MATERIALS

_____

_____

_____

_____

_____

_____

_____

_____

_____

PROCESS

Continued on page

NAME OF COURSE/TUTORIAL _____

TUTOR _____ EXPIRY DATE _____

LOCATION, web address,
computer folder, book etc _____

SOFTWARE (if applicable) _____

MATERIALS

_____
_____
_____
_____
_____
_____
_____
_____
_____

PROCESS

Continued on page

NAME OF COURSE/TUTORIAL _____

TUTOR _____ EXPIRY DATE _____

LOCATION, web address,
computer folder, book etc _____

SOFTWARE (if applicable) _____

MATERIALS

_____
_____
_____
_____
_____
_____
_____
_____
_____

PROCESS

Continued on page

NAME OF COURSE/TUTORIAL _____

TUTOR _____ EXPIRY DATE _____

LOCATION, web address,
computer folder, book etc   _____

SOFTWARE (if applicable)   _____

MATERIALS

_____
_____
_____
_____
_____
_____
_____
_____
_____
_____

PROCESS

Continued on page

NAME OF COURSE/TUTORIAL _____

TUTOR _____ EXPIRY DATE _____

LOCATION, web address,
computer folder, book etc   _____

SOFTWARE (if applicable)   _____

MATERIALS

_____

_____

_____

_____

_____

_____

_____

_____

_____

_____

PROCESS

Continued on page

NAME OF COURSE/TUTORIAL _____

TUTOR _____ EXPIRY DATE _____

LOCATION, web address,
computer folder, book etc _____

SOFTWARE (if applicable) _____

MATERIALS

_____

_____

_____

_____

_____

_____

_____

_____

_____

PROCESS

Continued on page

NAME OF COURSE/TUTORIAL _____

TUTOR _____ EXPIRY DATE _____

LOCATION, web address,
computer folder, book etc _____

SOFTWARE (if applicable) _____

MATERIALS

_____
_____
_____
_____
_____
_____
_____
_____
_____

PROCESS

Continued on page

NAME OF COURSE/TUTORIAL _____

TUTOR _____ EXPIRY DATE _____

LOCATION, web address,
computer folder, book etc   _____

SOFTWARE (if applicable)   _____

MATERIALS

_____
_____
_____
_____
_____
_____
_____
_____
_____

PROCESS

Continued on page

NAME OF COURSE/TUTORIAL _____

TUTOR _____ EXPIRY DATE _____

LOCATION, web address,
computer folder, book etc   _____

SOFTWARE (if applicable)   _____

MATERIALS

_____
_____
_____
_____
_____
_____
_____
_____
_____

PROCESS

_____
_____
_____
_____
_____
_____
_____
_____

Continued on page

NAME OF COURSE/TUTORIAL _____

TUTOR _____ EXPIRY DATE _____

LOCATION, web address,
computer folder, book etc _____

SOFTWARE (if applicable) _____

MATERIALS

_____
_____
_____
_____
_____
_____
_____
_____
_____
_____

PROCESS

Continued on page

NAME OF COURSE/TUTORIAL _____

TUTOR _____ EXPIRY DATE _____

LOCATION, web address,
computer folder, book etc   _____

SOFTWARE (if applicable)   _____

MATERIALS

_____

PROCESS

Continued on page

NAME OF COURSE/TUTORIAL _____

TUTOR _____ EXPIRY DATE _____

LOCATION, web address,
computer folder, book etc   _____

SOFTWARE (if applicable)   _____

MATERIALS

_____
_____
_____
_____
_____
_____
_____
_____
_____
_____

PROCESS

Continued on page

NAME OF COURSE/TUTORIAL _____

TUTOR _____ EXPIRY DATE _____

LOCATION, web address,
computer folder, book etc _____

SOFTWARE (if applicable) _____

MATERIALS

_____
_____
_____
_____
_____
_____
_____
_____
_____

PROCESS

Continued on page

NAME OF COURSE/TUTORIAL _____

TUTOR _____ EXPIRY DATE _____

LOCATION, web address,
computer folder, book etc   _____

SOFTWARE (if applicable) _____

MATERIALS

_____
_____
_____
_____
_____
_____
_____
_____
_____
_____

PROCESS

Continued on page

NAME OF COURSE/TUTORIAL _____

TUTOR _____ EXPIRY DATE _____

LOCATION, web address,
computer folder, book etc _____

SOFTWARE (if applicable) _____

MATERIALS

_____
_____
_____
_____
_____
_____
_____
_____
_____

PROCESS

Continued on page

NAME OF COURSE/TUTORIAL _____

TUTOR _____ EXPIRY DATE _____

LOCATION, web address,
computer folder, book etc _____

SOFTWARE (if applicable) _____

MATERIALS

_____
_____
_____
_____
_____
_____
_____
_____
_____

PROCESS

Continued on page

NAME OF COURSE/TUTORIAL _____

TUTOR _____ EXPIRY DATE _____

LOCATION, web address,
computer folder, book etc   _____

SOFTWARE (if applicable)   _____

MATERIALS

PROCESS

Continued on page

NAME OF COURSE/TUTORIAL _____

TUTOR _____ EXPIRY DATE _____

LOCATION, web address,
computer folder, book etc _____

SOFTWARE (if applicable) _____

MATERIALS

_____
_____
_____
_____
_____
_____
_____
_____
_____

PROCESS

Continued on page

NAME OF COURSE/TUTORIAL _____

TUTOR _____ EXPIRY DATE _____

LOCATION, web address,
computer folder, book etc _____

SOFTWARE (if applicable) _____

MATERIALS

_____

_____

_____

_____

_____

_____

_____

_____

_____

PROCESS

Continued on page

NAME OF COURSE/TUTORIAL _____

TUTOR _____ EXPIRY DATE _____

LOCATION, web address,
computer folder, book etc _____

SOFTWARE (if applicable) _____

MATERIALS

_____
_____
_____
_____
_____
_____
_____
_____
_____
_____

PROCESS

Continued on page

NAME OF COURSE/TUTORIAL _____

TUTOR _____ EXPIRY DATE _____

LOCATION, web address,
computer folder, book etc _____

SOFTWARE (if applicable) _____

MATERIALS

_____

_____

_____

_____

_____

_____

_____

_____

_____

PROCESS

Continued on page

NAME OF COURSE/TUTORIAL _____

TUTOR _____ EXPIRY DATE _____

LOCATION, web address,
computer folder, book etc _____

SOFTWARE (if applicable) _____

MATERIALS

PROCESS

Continued on page

NAME OF COURSE/TUTORIAL _____

TUTOR _____ EXPIRY DATE _____

LOCATION, web address,
computer folder, book etc   _____

SOFTWARE (if applicable)   _____

MATERIALS

_____

_____

_____

_____

_____

_____

_____

_____

_____

PROCESS

Continued on page

NAME OF COURSE/TUTORIAL _____

TUTOR _____ EXPIRY DATE _____

LOCATION, web address,
computer folder, book etc _____

SOFTWARE (if applicable) _____

MATERIALS

_____

_____

_____

_____

_____

_____

_____

_____

_____

PROCESS

Continued on page

NAME OF COURSE/TUTORIAL _____

TUTOR _____ EXPIRY DATE _____

LOCATION, web address,
computer folder, book etc _____

SOFTWARE (if applicable) _____

MATERIALS

_____

_____

_____

_____

_____

_____

_____

_____

_____

_____

PROCESS

Continued on page

NAME OF COURSE/TUTORIAL _____

TUTOR _____ EXPIRY DATE _____

LOCATION, web address,
computer folder, book etc   _____

SOFTWARE (if applicable)   _____

MATERIALS

_____
_____
_____
_____
_____
_____
_____
_____
_____

PROCESS

_____
_____
_____
_____
_____
_____
_____

Continued on page

www.ingramcontent.com/pod-product-compliance
Lightning Source LLC
Chambersburg PA
CBHW081003170526
45158CB00010B/2891